A THOUSAND YEARS

Kenny Finkle

BROADWAY PLAY PUBLISHING INC
224 E 62nd St, NY, NY 10065
www.broadwayplaypub.com
info@broadwayplaypub.com

First printing June 2014
I S B N: 978-0-88145-601-1

Book design: Marie Donovan
Page make-up: Adobe Indesign
Typeface: Palatino
Printed and bound in the U S A

A THOUSAND YEARS was originally presented as a work-in-progress by F I U Theatre, Miami, in its Alternative Theatre Festival in July 2013. The cast and creative contributors were:

MIRIAM..Michelle L Antelo

Ensemble ....Peter Mir
Patrick Rodriguez
Francesca Toledo

Director..Michael Yawney
Stage manager..Nelly Torres
Scenic & lighting design........................ Amanda Sparhawk
Costume design...Angie Esposito
Sound design.. Paul Steinsland

CHARACTERS

suggested breakdown:

MIRIAM

Male 1:
DOCTOR
COP
DIAMOND
DOCTOR 3
TONY
GARY GURU
HIRAM
and (sometimes the SHE DOCTOR*)*

Male 2:
MAN
DOCTOR 2
JACKSON
FLYER (*in France*)
JACQUES
UNCLE HARRY
DAVID

Female 2:
PATRICE
ALICE
LAURI
NELLA
AUNT MARILYN
SHE DOCTOR

NOTE

This play is a fairytale.

It should be done with minimal sets, costumes and props.

A NOTE ON STAGE DIRECTIONS

While developing and workshopping the play, the role of the stage directions in the play was continually being explored. It became clear that much of what is written in the stage directions need to be either said or presented as part of the production. This is because in the world of this play the stage directions, instead of the dialogue, often impart the most valuable information about what the characters are doing, where they are and how much time has passed.

In this way, I believe the stage directions are a character in the play.

How a production chooses to represent this is entirely open to possibility.

-This could be a voice over

-This could be a 5th actor

-This could be divided among the cast (as the workshop production in Miami did).

It may help to decide first though WHO is telling the story and then use the stage directions to support that vision.

Special Thanks
Wendy Dann, Michael Yawney
and Sheldon Allen

(Light up on the SHE DOCTOR. *She seems to be looking for something below her and very small. She holds a spinning top, poised to spin. The* SHE DOCTOR *leans in to see something as—light up on* MIRIAM JAMES, *early 30s, sitting in a hospital waiting room.)*

(The SHE DOCTOR *watches* MIRIAM *like a T V show.)*

MIRIAM: *(To herself/the heavens)* It's been five hours, twenty-two minutes and—forty-five seconds and no word. This is too long to bear. I don't know if I can wait another second.

SHE DOCTOR: Let's find out what you *can* bear Miriam James...
(A spell)
TIME SPIN SLOW
THEN SPEED
AND CAREEN
DESTROY ALL YOU KNOW
LET GO
FIND SERENE.
(She spins her spinning top.)

(We hear the sound of Time ticking.)

(The SHE DOCTOR's *light goes out.)*

(In MIRIAM's *world, a male* DOCTOR *enters, its clear he's just come right from surgery.)*

(He looks to MIRIAM.)*

(She stands.)

MIRIAM: How is he?

DOCTOR: He's in a coma.

MIRIAM: A coma?

DOCTOR: Yes.

MIRIAM: …

DOCTOR: We are unsure at this point if he's going to wake and if he—

MIRIAM: If?

DOCTOR: Yes if. …And if he does wake, what state he'll wake in.

MIRIAM: What state he'll wake in?

DOCTOR: We won't know. We don't know. You should go home. He's not going to wake up tonight.

MIRIAM: How do you know that?

DOCTOR: I don't. I just—

MIRIAM: No, I'll stay. I'll stay and I'll wait.

DOCTOR: Ok. Then maybe step out and get some air, get a coffee?

MIRIAM: With you?

DOCTOR: No, sorry, I wasn't—I didn't mean—I meant maybe you should do that. To get out for a little while.

MIRIAM: Oh. Right. That's—right. Good idea. Get out for a little bit. Right. O K.

———

(On the street about fifteen minutes later. MIRIAM is walking back to the Hospital, holding a large coffee.)

(We're in N Y C. Hustle and bustle. Sounds of the city)

(Quite suddenly, a MAN rushes up behind MIRIAM, grabs her, holds a knife to her neck.)

MIRIAM: Oh my god.

MAN: Shut up.

MIRIAM: O K.

MAN: You're coming with me.

MIRIAM: No. You don't understand my husband is—

MAN: I said—shut up! And I meant it! Jeez!

MIRIAM: Jeez?

MAN: Yeah! Jeez!

MIRIAM: Where are you taking me?

MAN: Wouldn't you like to know.

MIRIAM: Yeah. Yeah I would.

MAN: Shut up!

MIRIAM: Fine. Fine. Oh god. Fine. O K.

————

(In the back of a van. Hours later. MIRIAM is tied up leaning, passed out against the wall of the van. She sits across from PATRICE, tough broad. PATRICE is wide awake watching MIRIAM. MIRIAM stirs.)

MIRIAM: Where am—

PATRICE: You're in a van. I'm Patrice. You've been abducted. Knocked out. I've been abducted too.

MIRIAM: Abducted?

PATRICE: It's alright, you're foggy, you'll remember in a minute.

(Beat. MIRIAM thinks, she remembers.)

MIRIAM: Where is he taking us?

PATRICE: No clue. We've definitely left the city. Been in here for at least three hours. Maybe longer.

MIRIAM: Shit. Shit. Shit. David,

PATRICE: Who's David?

MIRIAM: My husband—

PATRICE: Probably called the Police by now.

MIRIAM: No. He's in a coma. I was just walking back from getting a coffee. The Doctor suggested that I—

PATRICE: Shit.

MIRIAM: I couldn't stand it if he woke up and I wasn't there.

PATRICE: We have to get you back to the Hospital. We'll have to make a break for it.

MIRIAM: O K. How?

PATRICE: Got me. Maybe if we open that back door, we can roll out?

MIRIAM: Into oncoming traffic.

PATRICE: Good point. When he comes to get us, we'll attack him. We'll fight him together, take the van and drive back to the city and you'll get back to David.

MIRIAM: Do you think we can do that? He's got a knife.

PATRICE: Yeah, I'm not sure, one of us may have to sacrifice themselves for the sake of the other.

MIRIAM: Oh.

PATRICE: I'll sacrifice myself..

MIRIAM: You'd really sacrifice yourself for me?

PATRICE: Yeah. You love David right?

MIRIAM: Yes. With all my being.

PATRICE: Then yeah, I'll help you in every way I can to get back to him.

MIRIAM: Thanks Patrice…

PATRICE: Nothing to thank me for. Shit, it'll be the noblest thing I've ever done.

MIRIAM: Really?

PATRICE: Yeah, I've lived a very dark life.

———

(Hours later. MIRIAM, covered in blood, now driving the van. She's alone, on her cell phone.)

MIRIAM: Hi. Hello. My husband is a patient there? David James. He's in a coma. Or he was when I left. I went out for coffee and was abducted, but I'm ok now. I'm wondering if he's O K. If he's—no, don't worry about me, it's all fine now, I just wonder if he's—O K, I'll hold. I'm holding.

(A COP siren in the background, it gets louder.)

MIRIAM: Shit. Shit. Shit.

COP: *(On loud speaker)* PULL OVER!

MIRIAM: O K! O K!!!!

COP: *(On loud speaker)* PUT DOWN THE CELL PHONE!

MIRIAM: I can't!

COP: *(On loud speaker)* PUT DOWN THE CELL PHONE OR I WILL SHOOT YOU!

MIRIAM: SHOOT ME?

COP: *(On loud speaker)* YES! SHOOT YOU!!!! FOR REAL!

MIRIAM: O K, O K, I'm just—I'm trying to find out what happened to my—

COP: *(On loud speaker)* THIS IS NOT A VIDEO GAME!

MIRIAM: I know that!

COP: *(On loud speaker)* I HAVE REAL BULLETS.

MIRIAM: O K, I just—Oh! Hello? Yes it's she.

(The COP fires a bullet. Startling MIRIAM)

MIRIAM: AH!!!! *(Into the phone)* I'm sorry what was that?

COP: *(On loud speaker)* THAT WAS A WARNING SHOT! THE NEXT SHOT GOES INTO YOUR BRAIN!

MIRIAM: Oh my god. Oh my god. Sorry I didn't hear that?

(Another gun shot. It breaks the glass on her windshield. MIRIAM screams and drops the phone.)

MIRIAM: Shit! Don't hang up! I'm coming! I just dropped the phone by accident! Hold on!

(MIRIAM tries to grab the phone off the floor of the van but can't keep her eyes on the road. She disappears for a second, when she pops her head back up—she sees something coming right towards her that looks like the SHE DOCTOR!!!!!)

MIRIAM: OH MY GOD WHAT IS THAT?

(Blackout)

(In the darkness, we hear a horrible crash)

———

(We're now in a hospital. A few days later. A different hospital. A different DOCTOR stands over MIRIAM who is tied to the bed. MIRIAM wakes up.)

DOCTOR: There you are.

MIRIAM: Where am I?

DOCTOR: In a hospital.

MIRIAM: What hospital?

DOCTOR: Baptist Presbyterian.

MIRIAM: Oh…who am I?

DOCTOR: I was hoping you'd be able to tell me.

MIRIAM: No clue.

DOCTOR: Oh dear.

MIRIAM: Don't I have any identification?

DOCTOR: None.

MIRIAM: I don't seem like the kind of person that wouldn't have identification.

DOCTOR: You also don't seem like the kind of person who would kill two people, but apparently you are.

MIRIAM: I am?

DOCTOR: Apparently so. That's why you're tied to the bed. You're considered a threat.

MIRIAM: To who?

DOCTOR: Society.

MIRIAM: Wow.

DOCTOR: Seriously.

MIRIAM: How did I apparently kill them?

DOCTOR: With a knife.

MIRIAM: Wow. I must be pretty strong.

DOCTOR: If you are, it's not apparent.

MIRIAM: What about fingerprints?

DOCTOR: All the skin on your fingers and toes was burned off in the accident.

MIRIAM: D N A?

DOCTOR: Inconclusive.

MIRIAM: That makes no sense.

DOCTOR: Does anything really?

MIRIAM: Uh—

DOCTOR: Well, O K, I suppose someone will come in and take you to jail or something soon.

MIRIAM: Jail?

DOCTOR: Yes.

MIRIAM: But I haven't even had a trial.

DOCTOR: Open and shut case, they said.

MIRIAM: But I don't know who I am.

DOCTOR: Do any of us?

MIRIAM: I'm so not in a position to enjoy a good existential question right now.

DOCTOR: But aren't you?

———

(Ten years later, MIRIAM in jail. She is in her cell with her cellmate—ALICE, little tough motherfucker. ALICE has a huge brick in her hand. She's standing over MIRIAM.)

ALICE: I don't know, I'm not sure this is a good idea Kid A.

MIRIAM: I hate when you call me Kid A.

ALICE: What about when I call you Jane Doe?

MIRIAM: I don't like that either but its better than Kid A.

ALICE: Well I'm not calling you Petula.

MIRIAM: Why not? It's the name I've chosen for myself.

ALICE: It's a shitty name.

MIRIAM: Well you won't have to use it again after you knock me on the head with that brick and I get my memory back.

ALICE: What if you get your memory back and your name really is Petula and you really did kill those people? That would be such a bummer. I mean, it'd be devastating. I'd just think—what's the point of going on?

MIRIAM: Alice. Shut up and hit me on the head. And you have to do it hard or it won't take.

ALICE: I just don't know if this is going to do anything.

MIRIAM: Just do it!

ALICE: O K, but first you have to sign this.

MIRIAM: What is it?

ALICE: It's a waiver. It frees me from any responsibility, in case you incur permanent brain damage or memory loss—well you already have that, but you know what I mean, I looked it up in the Prison Library.

MIRIAM: Fine. I'll sign it. Give me a pen.

ALICE: *(Handing her a pen)* Do you know that a lot of the Muslims hang out in the Library?

(MIRIAM *signs the paper.*)

MIRIAM: Ok. Now hit me. Now!

(ALICE *bangs* MIRIAM *on the head with the brick. Hard)*

MIRIAM: Ow! Fuck! FUCK!

ALICE: What's your name?

(Beat)

MIRIAM: Miriam.

ALICE: Miriam?

MIRIAM: Yeah. Miriam! I'm Miriam!

ALICE: Holy shit, it worked!

MIRIAM: Holy shit! And I have to get to my husband David, he's in the hospital, or he was—ten years ago, in a coma. I have to get to him.

ALICE: What should we do? Should we ask a Guard for help?

MIRIAM: Help with what?

ALICE: They could call the Hospital, they could find out if he's ok, where he is, whatever, I don't know.

MIRIAM: Yeah, let's do that. Let's see if they'll call the Hospital. Ok.

ALICE: GUARD! GUARD!!! GUARD!!!!

(*The guard,* DIAMOND *appears. She's played by a he and is kind of horribly scary.*)

DIAMOND: Whatch you two whores want neeeow?

ALICE: She remembers who she is.

MIRIAM: I'm Miriam.

DIAMOND: I's Diamond.

MIRIAM: I know. But you see Diamond, my husband, is in the hospital in a coma. Or was. He was in the hospital. He could still be. I know its unlikely ten years later but he could be. And I need to get to him. I need to find out if he's O K. It was touch and go so—

DIAMOND: You gotta husband? Sheeeeeit. Diamond can't keep a man to stay for a whole night and you got a husband. You're a damn murderer and you got a husband. Diamond pays her taxes, tries to eat low fat meals, use aspartame instead of regular sugar, Diamond always takes the stairs—when she's going up two or less flights, and you got a husband.

MIRIAM: Yes. But you see, I'm not really a murderer. I've been framed. I mean, I didn't do it. I remember everything now. And so don't hate me, I'm just like you.

DIAMOND: You and Diamond won't ever be alike. You know why?

MIRIAM: Why?

DIAMOND: Cuz you're gonna die in this shit hole and Diamond's gonna die in the Bahamas with a pina colada in her hand, mmmmmok? Peace. *(Walks off)*

MIRIAM: Wait! Diamond! Wait! Please! Well at least get me a lawyer! I deserve a lawyer for this! I have a case! I have my memory!

(From offstage)

DIAMOND: Diamond can't hear you. Diamond's got "Wheel of Fortune" on real loud.

MIRIAM: Shit! Now what am I gonna do? *(She sits on her "bed" devastated.)*

ALICE: Ummmm…Miriam?

MIRIAM: What?

ALICE: Ummmm…I wasn't gonna share this with you cuz I didn't know if you'd be cool with it.

MIRIAM: Cool with what?

ALICE: With this. *(She pulls back the sink to reveal a hole in the wall.)* I've been digging it every night for the past twenty years with this spork.

(ALICE reveals a spork out of a surprising place on her body. MIRIAM looks into the hole in the wall.)

———

(Later that night in the tunnel. The two women have been crawling for hours.)

MIRIAM: I can't believe you did all this with a spork.

ALICE: Yeah I know.

(ALICE *and* MIRIAM *come to a fork in the tunnel.*)

MIRIAM: Why is there a fork in this tunnel?

ALICE: Oh that. Yeah, I got confused and wasn't sure which way I was supposed to dig so I figured I'd just dig in both directions and figure it out later.

MIRIAM: So which direction should we go in?

ALICE: I haven't figured that out yet.

MIRIAM: But didn't you have a map or a plan when you set out to do this?

ALICE: No. I just dug.

MIRIAM: But—

ALICE: Don't worry Kid A—I mean Miriam, both of these go really far. So they won't end up anywhere near the prison.

MIRIAM: How far?

ALICE: I didn't really measure it or anything. But it should be fine.

(*From behind them, they hear—*)

DIAMOND: (*Offstage*) Diamond is behind you bitches. Diamond is crawling through this hole and is gonna get you!

MIRIAM: Oh shit. Shit. Shit. Shit.

ALICE: Don't worry, I have it taken care of.

(*Just then we hear—*)

DIAMOND: (*Offstage*) Ooh looks, Diamond sees herself a Mars bar. What's that doing down here? Diamond loves herself some Mars bars.

(*We hear what sounds like a huge crash.*)

MIRIAM: What was that sound?

ALICE: The sound of Diamond being taken care of.

MIRIAM: Oh my god.

ALICE: It was either her or us. So I'm thinking we should go left.

MIRIAM: O K. Left.

———

(Hours later, the two women are still crawling through the tunnel.)

MIRIAM: We met, in graduate school. Twelve, no, twenty two, god, twenty two years ago.

ALICE: You went to graduate school?

MIRIAM: Yes. We met there. We—

ALICE: What did you study?

MIRIAM: We both studied Philosophy. We were in the same class. We were friends. Buddies.

ALICE: I've never been a buddy with a man.

MIRIAM: It was easy in graduate school. We just talked Philosophy all the time. And he—David, he always had girlfriends so we were, it was easy to just be friends I guess…

ALICE: And you?

MIRIAM: Sometimes. Sometimes I had boyfriends. I wasn't as popular as David.

ALICE: Why was David so popular?

MIRIAM: Because he's the most amazing guy. He's funny, and smart and sarcastic and tender and incredibly honest. And generous. And loving. And surprising. And ambitious. And handsome. Did I mention how handsome he is? When he walks into a room, he literally takes my breath away.

(DAVID *appears. We're no longer in a tunnel.*)

DAVID: Hey babe.

MIRIAM: David!

(MIRIAM *rushes to him. They are about to kiss. Then—*)

ALICE: Ouch. Fuck. Ow!

(DAVID *disappears.*)

MIRIAM: Are you O K?

ALICE: Something bit me I think.

MIRIAM: Oh.

ALICE: Be careful. Anyway, so you two fell in love in graduate school?

MIRIAM: No, we didn't. We were friends in graduate school. Just friends. We hung out a lot but we were just friends.

ALICE: So when did you two get together then?

MIRIAM: A year before the accident.

ALICE: Just a year?

MIRIAM: Yeah. We'd lost touch after grad school. But then, five years later, we ran into each other at a bar.

(*We're now at the bar. Loud music. Lower East Side grungy.* MIRIAM *comes up to the bar to order a drink.* DAVID *is standing there.*)

DAVID: Miriam?

MIRIAM: David?

(*The two have an instant connection.* MIRIAM *turning back to the still tunneling* ALICE…)

MIRIAM: We exchanged numbers and a few weeks later got together for coffee.

(At a coffeeshop)

MIRIAM: So wait, you and Christine got married?

DAVID: Three years ago.

MIRIAM: How did I miss that?

DAVID: I have no idea. I wanted to invite you. I tried to find you. It seemed like you just kind of disappeared off the face of the Earth.

MIRIAM: No. Just moved to Queens.

DAVID: Same difference.

MIRIAM: Queens has its merits.

DAVID: I'm not yawning because I'm bored.

(MIRIAM punches DAVID in the arm. The two laugh. Beat)

MIRIAM: I missed you in my life David James.

DAVID: I missed you in my life Miriam Keenan.

MIRIAM: *(To ALICE)* We started meeting every few weeks. Then every couple weeks. Then every week. Then we had a standing date on Thursday nights. We had gotten into this habit of getting a bottle of wine and a pizza and sitting in the park by the East River and watching the sky.

(We're now at the East River. The two are watching the sky.)

DAVID: When I was little I wanted to be an astronaut.

MIRIAM: Don't all little boys want to be astronauts?

DAVID: Don't all little girls want to be know it alls?

MIRIAM: I didn't mean that to sound like I was belittling your childhood dreams.

DAVID: But—

MIRIAM: But come on! An astronaut?! Honestly David I would have expected more from you.

DAVID: Like what?

MIRIAM: I just assumed when you were a little boy you wanted to be Heidegger.

DAVID: Yeah, when I was five I was obsessed with German philosophy.

MIRIAM: Me too!

DAVID: Can I go on with what I wanted to tell you?

MIRIAM: Yes but first pass me another slice of the pizza please.

DAVID: Isn't that your fourth slice?

MIRIAM: Isn't that rude to point out?

DAVID: Where do you put all of it?

MIRIAM: Into my muscles, it makes me stronger. See?

(MIRIAM *punches* DAVID *in the arm.*)

DAVID: I'm wounded!

MIRIAM: Now pass me the pizza.

DAVID: First you have to listen to me.

MIRIAM: You're hijacking the pizza? Is that what's happening right now?

DAVID: Yes.

MIRIAM: Fine. Please tell me whatever it is you have to tell me.

DAVID: Now it seems stupid.

MIRIAM: Just tell me.

DAVID: I was just going to tell you about how when I was little I was obsessed with space. And that maybe, even if its cliché, I wanted to be an astronaut and I had this dream that one day I'd go up in space in a space ship and I'd float in space and I'd be all alone up there, in space, floating around and it'd be so quiet and large and mysterious and calm. That's mostly what I'd think about it—that it'd be calm. Sometimes now when I'm at work or at home recently and I can't take another second of it, I think about that. About the calm. And it calms me. I think of it as my antidote.

MIRIAM: Antidote to what?

DAVID: To everything. Except you. When I'm with you I feel calm. Like nothing else matters.

(Beat)

MIRIAM: That's when it hit me that we loved each other. That the great affection, the charge, the easiness, the joy, the thoughtfulness, the instant understanding was the true definition of love and in that moment I had this very clear vision of a life with him. I could see it stretching out in front of me, like a beautiful, luxurious piece of fabric and it just expanded and grew and flowed. And so I turned to him. And I said— David—but before I could get more out, he said—

DAVID: Christine left me this morning. *(He starts to cry.)*

MIRIAM: Oh David.

(MIRIAM grabs DAVID and holds him.)

MIRIAM: I'm so sorry. I'm so sorry this happened to you. You don't deserve this. You don't deserve to feel pain. You deserve love. I—I could love you the way you're supposed to be loved. I could.

DAVID: What are you—

MIRIAM: David I love you. I love you and I think you love me. I think this is love. Haven't you ever felt like this is—

DAVID: But we're friends Miriam.

MIRIAM: I know but we don't have to be. I mean, we can be more than just friends. We could—We could just be who we are right now to each other. Our love could be just an extension of this. Of what we already have. We could—

DAVID: This is—too soon for me. This isn't—we're friends Miriam. And—

MIRIAM: I know we are and I wouldn't have said any of this if I didn't feel like you felt this way too. Don't you see it? If you're scared, that's ok, I'm scared too. Love is scary. If its courage you need, we can find that together. We can—

DAVID: But I need you to be my friend right now. I need you to help me. I need you to—

MIRIAM: I can't. I want to be. I want to be just your friend but I can't. *(To ALICE)* We stopped talking after that. I was stupid and selfish and I shouldn't have said anything but I couldn't wait. I felt like time was suddenly moving so fast and if I didn't say anything then maybe I would never say anything… Six months passed and nothing. I figured I had to move on. I started to date but I wouldn't really let anyone get close and I realized that, as cheesy as this sounds, that I really had to let go of David, in order to give myself over to someone else. So that night, I sat by the East River, watching the sky and said goodbye to David. I let him go. And then the next morning, I kid you not, I was on my way out the door and David was standing there waiting for me.

DAVID: You have a few minutes?

MIRIAM: *(To ALICE)* Of course I did.

DAVID: Last night I—I went to the East River and I was sitting there looking at the stars and something—lifted out of me and for the first time I could really see you, who you are to me, who you could be to me. And I could see our life together, it stretched out in front of me, I could see it all. I can't live without you. These six months have been—without meaning. I'm sorry. I'm sorry it took me so long. Am I too late?

MIRIAM: I kissed him. He came inside. We made love. We were married a month later.

ALICE: That's—that's so—

(*Beat.* ALICE *grabs her heart. Has trouble breathing. And then quite suddenly dies.*)

MIRIAM: What about you? Do you have someone special in your life? (*Silence*) Alice?

(MIRIAM *turns around and sees* ALICE.)

———

(*A day later.* MIRIAM *crawls out of a hole in the Earth. We're on a beach.*)

MIRIAM: The beach? How did she tunnel all the way to the ocean?

(JACKSON, *a hermit, scraggly, weather-beaten and coarse rushes up to her.*)

JACKSON: I saw that. I saw you. You climbed out of the Earth. Are you a creature from the underworld?

MIRIAM: What? No. I'm Miriam.

JACKSON: Miriam. How'd you do that?

MIRIAM: It's a long story. Where am I?

JACKSON: Nova Scotia.

MIRIAM: Nova Scotia?

JACKSON: Nova Scotia. I'm Jackson. You smell horrible.

MIRIAM: I know I do.

JACKSON: I bet you could use a shower.

MIRIAM: Yes. And a phone. I could use a phone most of all.

JACKSON: The shower I got. The phone I don't.

MIRIAM: You don't have a phone?

JACKSON: Naw. I'm a hermit. Shut myself off from the world. No way to make contact with me. But you seem pretty interesting—crawling out from the Earth. I had to take a gander at you up close. Come on, I'll give you a shower. And some food.

MIRIAM: Where's the nearest phone?

JACKSON: I'm sure somewhere in town.

MIRIAM: Where's town?

JACKSON: You've just been through some kind of ordeal. You need to eat and wash. Then we'll find you a phone.

MIRIAM: But I need a phone.

JACKSON: I promise we'll get you a phone as soon as you're cleaned up and fed some.

MIRIAM: Promise?

JACKSON: Cross my heart, hope to die, stick a needle in my eye. So what do you say?

MIRIAM: I *am* hungry.

JACKSON: Come on then.

———

(In JACKSON's *home. He lives in a lighthouse. An hour later.* MIRIAM's *been showered and sitting at a table eating.)*

JACKSON: So that's why you need a phone.

MIRIAM: Yeah.

JACKSON: We'll get you one. In the morning. You need to rest. How's the food?

MIRIAM: The food is fantastic. Thank you.

JACKSON: You're welcome. I've been dying to try out this recipe but haven't had occasion. Can you taste the basil in it?

MIRIAM: Yeah. And the fresh oregano.

JACKSON: Yes. And cilantro.

MIRIAM: I love cilantro.

JACKSON: I grow some in the back. I have a whole garden back there.

MIRIAM: I've never met anyone who lived in a lighthouse before.

JACKSON: Well now you have. I figured it fit my profile. Being a hermit and all.

MIRIAM: It does. It suits you.

JACKSON: I used to live in Syracuse.

MIRIAM: New York?

JACKSON: Yeah. It about killed me. I had to escape. So I did. Been up here going on forty years.

MIRIAM: Forty years?

JACKSON: You're the first person I've spoken to in close to fifteen. And that's only because I thought you were supernatural.

MIRIAM: Sorry to disappoint you.

JACKSON: Not at all. I'd forgotten that there were people like you in the world.

MIRIAM: People like me?

JACKSON: Good people.

MIRIAM: Oh, I'm not good.

JACKSON: Yes you are. You've got a good heart.

MIRIAM: So do you.

JACKSON: Bah Humbug. *(He smiles at* MIRIAM. *He pours her more wine.)*

———

(The next day. We're at a gas station on the side of the road. MIRIAM *is on a pay phone.* JACKSON *watches from his car.)*

MIRIAM: Oh that's wonderful. No not that he's—that he's there. Yes. I'll be there. As soon as I can. *(She hangs up. Walks to* JACKSON)

JACKSON: Well?

MIRIAM: He's still there. Still in a coma.

JACKSON: Mixed blessing I suppose.

MIRIAM: So now all I have to do is get back to New York.

JACKSON: Easy Breezy!

MIRIAM: I don't suppose you could lend me some money for a bus ticket?

JACKSON: I'll do better than that. I'll fly you.

MIRIAM: Fly me?

JACKSON: Got myself a little puddle jumper, named Easy Breezy, been dying to use her, just haven't had occasion.

MIRIAM: Oh. Well, are you a good pilot?

JACKSON: I was when I took lessons.

MIRIAM: How long ago was that?

JACKSON: Well let's see, been out here forty years, I took those lessons about forty-one years ago but I remember mostly everything I learned.

———

(A few hours later. In the sky. JACKSON *flies enjoying it immensely.* MIRIAM *holds on for dear life.)*

MIRIAM: *(Terror)* AHHHHHH!!!!!!!!!!!!!!!!!!!!!!!!!!!!!!!!!!!!!!!

JACKSON: *(Thrill)* YEEEEEHAAAAWWWWWWW!!!!!!!!

———

(A couple hours later. In a hospital room)

(The bed is made. Its empty. JACKSON *and* MIRIAM *stare at the bed. Behind them we see the* SHE DOCTOR *casually stroll by with a body in a wheelchair. She looks at* MIRIAM, *who doesn't see her.)*

MIRIAM: Where could he have gone? They said he was here. That he was still in a coma. Do you think he—

JACKSON: No. No Miriam. He's alive. Maybe they moved him somewhere else. Maybe he's—being given a bath or something.

(A DOCTOR *enters.)*

DOCTOR: Oh hello. Can I help you?

MIRIAM: We're looking for David. David James.

DOCTOR: Oh. Yeah, he just was released.

MIRIAM: He was? When?

DOCTOR: I don't know, maybe two, three minutes ago?

MIRIAM: He woke up?

DOCTOR: Nope. But a Doctor came in, said they were moving him to somewhere else.

MIRIAM: To where?

DOCTOR: Come to think of it, she didn't say.

MIRIAM: She?

DOCTOR: She. It was a She doctor.

———

(Soon after, JACKSON *and* MIRIAM *wandering the streets of N Y C.)*

MIRIAM: A She Doctor? Why would a She Doctor take David away?

(Just then a WOMAN *runs by and tries to take* MIRIAM'*s purse.)*

JACKSON: It's the She Doctor!

*(*JACKSON *jumps on top of the* WOMAN, *pinning her to the street.)*

WOMAN: You're strong!

JACKSON: Ever been hog tied little lady?

WOMAN: Once.

JACKSON: Really?

WOMAN: Totally...GET OFF ME NOW!!!!!

JACKSON: NOT ON YOUR LIFE SHE DOCTOR!

WOMAN: She Doctor? Who's the She Doctor?

MIRIAM: Lauri?

LAURI: Miriam?

———

(In a coffee shop. JACKSON, LAURI *and* MIRIAM *sit sipping tea.)*

JACKSON: I can't believe you two are cousins!

LAURI: I know, right?

JACKSON: Sorry for jumping on you like that.

LAURI: That's alright. I liked it. ...Miriam, I can't apologize enough for trying to steal your purse. I've just hit some bad luck and taken to thievery, it's nothing personal. I'm a good person. Deep down. You know I am. And I'm sorry no one in the family ever really looked for you enough. We did look. We looked a lot but then we kind of just got tired of looking and

MIRIAM: It's alright Lauri.

LAURI: I'm just overcome with guilt.

MIRIAM: Don't be.

LAURI: I'm wracked with it. I'm suffocating from it.

JACKSON: Lauri. Shut up.

LAURI: Right.

MIRIAM: So...what do I do now?

JACKSON: **We** find this She Doctor.

———

(Montage sequence!)

(We see JACKSON, MIRIAM *and* LAURI *in* JACKSON's *plane.* JACKSON *is enjoying himself.* MIRIAM *and* LAURI *are horrified.)*

(The three standing in front of a huge map, figuring out which way to go.)

(The pages of a calendar flying off—years and years are going by...)

(The SHE DOCTOR *watches* MIRIAM, LAURI *and* JACKSON *climbing the side of a mountain. The* SHE DOCTOR *makes a sudden movement and a great wind throws* MIRIAM, *she almost falls. The* SHE DOCTOR *laughs maniacally.* JACKSON *pulls* MIRIAM *back up.)*

(More pages of the calendar fly off.)

––––––

(Eighteen years later)

(On the streets of Dubai. MIRIAM with JACKSON, who is looking much older—feeble and LAURI who is much older too, but not feeble.)

LAURI: Dubai is the weirdest place on Earth.

MIRIAM: It's like some kind of simulation of reality.

LAURI: I want to live here.

JACKSON: No you don't.

LAURI: You're right. I don't. You know me so well.

JACKSON: Yes I do.

(The two look at each other—a smile.)

MIRIAM: We're almost there.

LAURI: Almost where?

MIRIAM: To the phone the She Doctor was last seen at. And according to this map, the phone should be right—over there.

(A pay phone is illuminated on stage.)

MIRIAM: That's it. That's the place she was last seen.

LAURI: It's a pay phone.

MIRIAM: I know that.

LAURI: So she could be anywhere.

MIRIAM: I know but she was here.

LAURI: But she's not now.

MIRIAM: That's not the point.

LAURI: It's the entire point. She and David could be anywhere now. Anywhere! Don't you get this Miriam? For the last eighteen years we've traveled the entire world—twice—trying to track down this stupid She Doctor and really, when we get somewhere its so obvious—she could be anywhere. We don't know enough about her to know how close or far we are. We don't know anything except that she's a She Doctor. Wasted! All of this. These eighteen years wasted.

JACKSON: I wouldn't say they've been completely wasted Lauri.

MIRIAM: No. She's right. This is a waste of time. A fool's journey. Its time to pack it in and go home.

(Just then the SHE DOCTOR *speeds by on a bike. There is clearly an unconscious man on the bike too. He's covered in a blanket. The* SHE DOCTOR *and* MIRIAM *make eye contact. The* SHE DOCTOR *winks…)*

MIRIAM: That's her! Did you see her? That's her! And that was David. David. He's right there. We have to follow her.

*(*JACKSON *whistles loudly. A* DUBAI BIKER *appears. The three jump on.)*

JACKSON: Follow that bike!

(They start to take off.)

JACKSON: No, not that bike—that bike, the one over there.

(They take off in the other direction.)

———

(An hour later, at the Dubai airport runway. JACKSON, MIRIAM *and* LAURI *rush onto the runway.)*

MIRIAM: There she is!

JACKSON: She's stuffing him onto a plane!

LAURI: This is so scary!

MIRIAM: We have to stop her!

(MIRIAM *starts to move forward. Gun shots. The* SHE
DOCTOR *is shooting at them.*)

MIRIAM: That fucking bitch!

(*We hear a plane taking off.*)

MIRIAM: She's taking off!

JACKSON: I wish I had my tomahawk right about now.

LAURI: You have a tomahawk?

JACKSON: Yup. It's back at the hotel. If we get back
there, I'll show it to you.

LAURI: Really?

MIRIAM: Jackson, get your plane.

JACKSON: My plane's in the shop. Mechanical
difficulties.

MIRIAM: Then steal one. We got to follow her.

JACKSON: Its bad luck to steal someone's plane.

MIRIAM: Please Jackson—David is on that plane.

———

(*A few hours later on the plane.* JACKSON *flies,* LAURI *sits
next to* JACKSON. MIRIAM *sits behind.*)

MIRIAM: You can't go any faster?

JACKSON: This isn't like mine Miriam, I'm doing my
best.

MIRIAM: But we've lost her. I can't see her. How do we know where she went?

LAURI: Miriam, he said he's doing his best. It's enough.

MIRIAM: No it's enough out of you.

LAURI: No it's enough out of you!

(LAURI *pulls* MIRIAM's *hair.*)

LAURI: Back off! Or you're gonna get popped off, understand?

JACKSON: Ladies! Enough already. It's enough. Tensions are high. A little argument is understandable. But it's enough already. Lauri I appreciate very much you trying to protect me. It means a great deal to me.

LAURI: It does?

JACKSON: Of course it does. Everything you do means a great deal to me.

LAURI: It does?

JACKSON: Of course it does. You're my reason for living Lauri. You're the woman of my dreams. You're my purpose. My soul. My heart. You drew me out of my hermit-hood.

MIRIAM: That was me. I did that. Not Lauri.

JACKSON: You've made me whole.

LAURI: Oh Jackson! JACKSON! JACKSON!!!!

(LAURI *plants a big one on* JACKSON's *face and hugs him hard. So hard the plane swerves.*)

ALL THREE: Whoa!

LAURI: Sorry.

JACKSON: Don't do that again Lauri. Not in the plane at least.

LAURI: Oh Jackson!

(JACKSON *and* LAURI *passionately kiss. The plane swerves again.*)

ALL THREE: Whoa!!

MIRIAM: Eyes on the sky! Eyes on the sky!

(JACKSON *goes back to flying. He and* LAURI *sneak a look at each other. A smile between them.*)

(*Everything seems fine.*)

(*Then—*)

(*The* SHE DOCTOR *appears next to* JACKSON. *They make eye contact. She blows him a kiss and is gone.*)

JACKSON: Did you see that?

MIRIAM: See what?

(*Just then the engines seem to cut out completely.*)

JACKSON: Oh shit.

MIRIAM: What is it?

JACKSON: Total engine failure. We're about to go down. Fast.

(JACKSON, LAURI *and* MIRIAM *all look at each other as we—*)

———

(*In the ocean.* MIRIAM *finds herself floating in the middle of the Ocean, holding onto a piece of the plane.* JACKSON *and* LAURI *float by, dead in a lover's embrace.* MIRIAM *watches them, then—*)

MIRIAM: (*To no one in particular and not very loud*) Help.

———

(Sixty five years later. MIRIAM *floats on the piece of the plane. She's exhausted.)*

MIRIAM: How is it possible that I've been on the ocean for sixty five years? How have I survived? How is it possible that I've not seen land?

(A message in a bottle floats by MIRIAM. *She picks it up. Takes out the message and reads.)*

MIRIAM: "Dear Larry, why didn't I ever tell you how much I loved you, if you find this, find me, Larue…".

(Just then a great tsunami appears behind MIRIAM. *She turns around and sees it. In the tsunami we can see the face of the* SHE DOCTOR *illuminated.)*

MIRIAM: You gotta be kidding me.

———

(A hundred years later MIRIAM *is swimming— determined—through the ocean. She passes another bottle. Stops and opens the bottle.)*

MIRIAM: *(Out of breath)* "Myrna, its Tony—where are you? Come home baby and let me sing to you".

*(*MIRIAM *puts the message back in the bottle and lets it go in the ocean as she swims on.)*

———

(Another hundred years. MIRIAM *is still swimming.* NELLA, *comfortable in her skin, regal, on a raft paddles up to* MIRIAM. *Her boat is covered with bottles, like the ones* MIRIAM *has seen—hundreds and hundreds of bottles.)*

NELLA: Hello.

MIRIAM: Hi.

NELLA: Give me your hand.

(MIRIAM *does and* NELLA *helps her on board. As* MIRIAM *catches her breath,* NELLA *looks hard at her, then—)*

NELLA: Two hundred and fifty years.

MIRIAM: Pardon?

NELLA: Two hundred and fifty years. I figure you've been out here for at least two hundred and fifty years.

MIRIAM: Actually it's been two hundred and sixty-five years.

NELLA: I was close! I'm Nella.

MIRIAM: Miriam.

NELLA: Four hundred and eighty two.

MIRIAM: Four hundred and eighty two what?

NELLA: Years. Out here. Looking.

MIRIAM: Really?

NELLA: Yes.

MIRIAM: How'd you know that I—

NELLA: You just start to notice.

MIRIAM: You have so many bottles.

NELLA: Yes.

MIRIAM: I keep opening them, hoping one will be from my husband.

NELLA: Yes, I know that feeling.

MIRIAM: Was your husband taken too?

NELLA: My husband's name is Theresa. Are you ok with that?

MIRIAM: With what? That you have a husband with a woman's name?

NELLA: No. That I'm gay.

MIRIAM: I'm horrified. Just kidding. Some of my best friends... I lived in Manhattan for a long time. I'm a liberal. I use to love smoking pot, when it was available to me. I love dance music. I made out with a girl in college. Actually we felt each other up too and we weren't even drunk. I used to watch that show *The L Word* on Showtime. So does that make you feel comfortable?

NELLA: Yes. It does.

MIRIAM: My husband's name is David. The She Doctor abducted him. I want to find him but I can't seem to find land.

NELLA: I can't either.

MIRIAM: Was Theresa abducted by the She Doctor too?

NELLA: I don't know. Maybe. She just disappeared so, I don't know what happened to her. *(Beat)* Should we travel together for a while?

————

(One hundred and fifty two years later. NELLA, MIRIAM *and another raft full of bottles and messages, this one with* TONY, *eternally stoned, on it, float in the ocean together. He has a guitar. He sings.)*

TONY: Tony *(Singing)*
You wake up on your right side
You tell me to look on the bright side
You hold me all night when I cry
You tell me you'll be there when I die

You make me the most delicious treats
You always laugh when i complain about my feet
You think when I get angry its sweet
You told me you predicted we'd meet

Where I leave off you pick up
When its empty you fill my cup
Why you do these things I'll never know
That's a secret that just grows and grows and grows
and grows and grows
I wrote that song for Myrna. For her birthday. That's
when she vanished. Well, right before her birthday, so
I never got to sing it to her.

(Beat)

MIRIAM: *(Seeing something)* Oh my god.

NELLA: What?

MIRIAM: Look!

TONY: Is that—

NELLA: It can't be.

MIRIAM: It is! It is!

ALL THREE: Land.

———

*(In Brest, France. A few days later. The world is like a
futuristic movie like* Blade Runner.*)*

(MIRIAM, NELLA, TONY are taken aback by it all.)

MIRIAM: Things have really changed.

NELLA: Seriously. Whoa! Watch out!

(Something low and fast zooms right over them.)

NELLA: Watch where you're going buddy!

FLYER: *(O S) Foutre le camp!*

NELLA: What did he just say?

MIRIAM: He said "Fuck off" in French.

TONY: You know French?

MIRIAM: Yeah. I studied it in high school and college.

NELLA: Well la di da...

TONY: I'm hungry.

MIRIAM: Me too.

NELLA: We don't have any money.

TONY: We have our bottles. We could try to bring them in for recycling.

NELLA: Do you think people still recycle?

———

(At the Recycling Place. A few hours later. The three are standing in front of JACQUES, *the Recycling Guy.)*

JACQUES: Bon jour! *(Inspecting their bottles)* These are very nice bottles. Very expensive. Not normal bottles. No! They are bottles made special. For a special person. A beautiful mademoiselle. A rich mademoiselle. A mysterious mademoiselle. An evil mademoiselle.

MIRIAM: Evil? How so?

JACQUES: Some say she steals loved ones.

MIRIAM: Tell me, just out of curiosity, what name does this mademoiselle go by?

JACQUES: The She Doctor!

(Thunder and lightning!)

MIRIAM & NELLA: The She Doctor?

(Thunder and lightning!)

JACQUES: Yes, the She Doctor!

(Thunder and lightning!)

TONY: I hate the rain. It scares me.

MIRIAM: Where does this She Doctor live?

JACQUES: High up in the highest mountains of Switzerland,

MIRIAM: O K.

JACQUES: There you will find a staircase to a man made elevation center three hundred and ninety-two thousand feet in the air. It is said that one can touch the atmosphere there. It is said that the atmosphere tastes like jolly ranchers. I like that it does.

MIRIAM: O K, so we go to the mountains of Switzerland, take the stairs to the elevation center and that's where the She Doctor lives..

JACQUES: No. From there, you charter a space ship that takes you deep into outer space.

TONY: Really?

JACQUES: No! I'm pulling your leg!!!! HAHAHAHA-HAHAHAHHAHAHAHAHAH!!! No, the She Doctor lives in a big castle on the Elevation Center. Or so its been said.

MIRIAM: Thank you.

JACQUES: But wait, I am forgetting something, a warning—Beware the air.

NELLA: Beware the air?

JACQUES: Yes. Beware the air. ...I'll give you twelve francs for all the bottles.

———

(In the Swiss Alps. Six months later. MIRIAM, NELLA *and* TONY *have climbed to the staircase. They are standing at the foot of it, looking up.)*

MIRIAM: Here it is. The staircase. Let's go you guys.

TONY: It goes really high up.

NELLA: And there's no railing.

TONY: And the stairs look like they're made of glass.

NELLA: Polished glass. Jacques didn't tell us about this. This is dangerous.

TONY: I'm afraid.

MIRIAM: No one said this was going to be easy. Let's go.

(MIRIAM *puts her foot on the first stair as we blackout.*)

———

(*A half hour later on the stairs*)

(*The three are taking slow, methodical steps.*)

(TONY *mis-steps and falls.* MIRIAM *and* NELLA *stop, turn and watch as he plummets to his death.*)

(*We hear the entire thing.*)

———

(*Six months later*)

(MIRIAM *and* NELLA *are sitting down on the stairs, trying to catch their breath.*)

MIRIAM: I can't catch my breath. The air, it's so

NELLA: Thin. Beware the Air!

MIRIAM: This is a trick?

NELLA: It must be.

MIRIAM: I don't think I can go on.

NELLA: We have to go on.

MIRIAM: I can't.

NELLA: You have to. Come on.

(NELLA *pulls* MIRIAM *up, they start to climb again.*)

(*Fifteen years later. Still on the stairs. Exhausted—*)

MIRIAM: I don't even remember who I'm looking for anymore.

NELLA: David. You're on your way to get David back.

MIRIAM: I don't remember what he looks like.

NELLA: You'll know him when you see him.

MIRIAM: I don't know if I love him anymore.

NELLA: You will when you see him.

MIRIAM: I don't know that I will.

NELLA: It's the air. Playing tricks. Don't give in. Don't listen to the voice in your own head.

MIRIAM: What if I've been searching all this time for someone I don't even really love?

NELLA: Your love for David is what's kept you alive. Do you hear me Miriam? Miriam?

MIRIAM: I want to forget about him. Forget everything. Just forget and be happy. Or relatively happy. Goodbye Nella. I'm giving up now. (*She jumps off the stairs.*)

NELLA: NO!

(*The* SHE DOCTOR *appears looking down on them. She laughs maniacally!*)

(A millisecond later. MIRIAM *falling through the sky.)*

MIRIAM: Forgive me David, forgive me for wanting to forget. For giving up. Forgive me for free falling. Forgive me for falling faster and faster, as fast as I can until I crash into the earth. And then—nothing. Nothing at all. I'll be nothing. A speck. Crash. Forgive me for forgetting. Forgive me.

———

(110 years later, MIRIAM, *is in a bed in a lush bedroom. She wakes with a start.* AUNT MARILYN *is sitting in a chair reading a book. She sees* MIRIAM *is up.)*

AUNT MARILYN: Oh you're up.

MIRIAM: Aunt Marilyn.

AUNT MARILYN: Hi.

MIRIAM: What are you doing here?

AUNT MARILYN: Watching you sleep and reading this wonderful book. Its called "Hopeless" and it's about a man who's name is Hiram, which is funny, you know I had a second cousin named Hiram, Hiram Hockney, he was a carny, worked carnivals all around the world, I always liked him, he was a funny guy that Hiram, not the Hiram in the book, the Hiram in the book, is not funny, this book is not funny, I wish it were a little funny, but its not, its more unrelenting, depressing, you know I like depressing literature, I always have, I don't know why, I like to know that people in the world, even if they're fictional have horrible lives, I like to know every detail of their miserable existence, I like to delve into their darkness and take a swim. Anyway, this is a really long book, I've been reading it for years and years, I love that about this book, its practically non ending but I'm almost at the end now,

are you hungry? I have some cookies I baked last night.
All your favorites are out, including the sugar cookies,
I still make those sugar cookies, you were always my
most favorite person to give those cookies to, they're
really wonderful cookies, do you want one, I'll get
you one, in a minute, you're still trying to catch your
breath. You're here now though and things here are
wonderful. This is an oasis. Isn't that wonderful? Your
Uncle—

MIRIAM: Uncle Harry?

AUNT MARILYN: Yeah, Harry's in the back fixing up the
pool so you can go for a swim. When you got here a
few days ago, we didn't have the heat on. Its on now.
Or it will be. HARRY!!!!????

HARRY: (O S) What?

AUNT MARILYN: Miriam's awake! Is the pool ready for
her?

HARRY: (O S) WHAT?

AUNT MARILYN: MIRIAM'S AWAKE!!!!! IS THE POOL
READY FOR HER?

HARRY: (O S) NO! BUT I'LL COME IN TO SAY
HELLO!

AUNT MARILYN: FIX THE POOL FIRST!

HARRY: (O S) WHAT?

AUNT MARILYN: I SAID FIX THE POOL FIRST AND
THEN COME IN!!!!

HARRY: (O S) BUT I WANT TO SEE HER!!!

AUNT MARILYN: AND I WANT THE POOL FIXED!!!!!
… (To MIRIAM) You're uncle. I can't live with him, I
can't live with him! Not like you and David, you and
David, that's a man to live with. That's a man to live
for. Where is he? Why isn't he here with you?

MIRIAM: Who?

AUNT MARILYN: David. Your husband.

MIRIAM: David. Oh I—I don't know.

AUNT MARILYN: What do you mean you don't know? What don't you know?

MIRIAM: Where David is. I—I lost him somewhere.

AUNT MARILYN: Lost him? I lost Harry somewhere once. Took me ninety years to find him but I found him. He was standing outside the T C B Y in Marlton, New Jersey, said he had been waiting for me to bring the car around. The yogurt melted he said. I didn't care. You should find David.

MIRIAM: I should. I was trying to. I gave up. I—

AUNT MARILYN: Why?

MIRIAM: It was too hard.

AUNT MARILYN: Life is hard Miriam. No way around that.

MIRIAM: I wasn't strong enough to get to the She Doctor.

AUNT MARILYN: Why not?

MIRIAM: I—I don't know.

AUNT MARILYN: When you were growing up you were the strongest girl I'd ever known. Resilient. So why aren't you now? You've gone this far. No reason to give up now. Right?

MIRIAM: But—

AUNT MARILYN: Right?

(Beat)

MIRIAM: Right.

AUNT MARILYN: Good.

MIRIAM: Aunt Marilyn?

AUNT MARILYN: Yeah?

MIRIAM: What am I doing here?

AUNT MARILYN: What, you're not happy to see me?

MIRIAM: No I am, I'm just wondering how I got here.

AUNT MARILYN: Oh. Well that's easy. ...You're not here at all darling, I'm a mirage.

MIRIAM: A mirage?

AUNT MARILYN: Yeah, happens all the time in the desert.

(AUNT MARILYN *gets up with the book and disappears. The bed turns into sand.*)

(MIRIAM *stands in the middle of a vast desert, nothing but sand for as far as the eye can see.*)

MIRIAM: How do I find my way to you? I have to find my way to you. I have to. *(She starts to walk. Looking)*

———

(92 years later, MIRIAM *is still wandering in the desert. She has been transformed. A shell of the woman she once was.)*

(She comes across GARY GURY, *who is sitting cross legged on the sand, meditating.)*

MIRIAM: Are you a mirage?

GARY GURU: That is a difficult question Miriam.

MIRIAM: How do you know my name?

GARY GURU: How do you know mine?

MIRIAM: I don't. Gary Guru. I do.

GARY GURU: How do you know mine?

MIRIAM: I just do.

GARY GURU: There's your answer. Come and sit Miriam.

MIRIAM: I can't sit. I have to get out of this desert.

GARY GURU: You've been wandering for almost a hundred years in this desert, five minutes with me won't kill you.

(MIRIAM *thinks this through and then sits. Beat*)

GARY GURU: You're getting old.

MIRIAM: I am.

GARY GURU: Why?

MIRIAM: I don't know.

GARY GURU: Yes you do.

MIRIAM: I can't find my way out.

GARY GURU: Why?

MIRIAM: Because I'm lost.

GARY GURU: Yes. Why are you lost?

MIRIAM: Because I can't find my way out.

GARY GURU: Yes. What do you need?

MIRIAM: I need help.

GARY GURU: I will help you. I will teach you how to get to the She Doctor. The rest you must do on your own.

MIRIAM: Thank you.

GARY GURU: No worries. This is a pleasure like a hamburger.

MIRIAM: Like a hamburger?

GARY GURU: I just wanted to let you know I had eaten a hamburger. And it was delicious. I got one in Burger King. I love fast food.

MIRIAM: I'd have thought you only eat organic.

GARY GURU: What's the point of organic?

MIRIAM: I don't know.

GARY GURU: Yes you do.

MIRIAM: To charge people more for their food.

GARY GURU: Yes. *(Beat. He looks at* MIRIAM.*)*

(The following section until indicated otherwise, is in voice over.)

GARY GURU: Speak the truth now Miriam.

MIRIAM: Are we talking in our minds right now?

GARY GURU: Yes.

MIRIAM: Wow.

GARY GURU: Cool, right?

MIRIAM: Yes.

GARY GURU: Speak the truth now.

MIRIAM: I thought my love for David was enough.

GARY GURU: It's not enough to love.

MIRIAM: What else do I need?

GARY GURU: Do you really want it?

MIRIAM: Yes.

GARY GURU: I don't believe you.

MIRIAM: I do.

GARY GURU: I still don't believe you.

MIRIAM: What can I do to convince you?

GARY GURU: It's not me you have to convince.

MIRIAM: What do I have to do to convince myself?

GARY GURU: Stand here for one hundred and thirty years without moving a muscle.

MIRIAM: What will that prove?

GARY GURU: You've proven you can look, now you must prove you can find.

(The telepathy spell is broken, the two speak to each other now.)

MIRIAM: What the hell does that mean?

GARY GURU: Just what I said.

MIRIAM: I hate spiritual gurus.

GARY GURU: Me too. *(Handing* MIRIAM *a strange root, looks like ginger)* Here take this.

MIRIAM: What is it?

GARY GURU: A hallucinogen.

MIRIAM: I don't—

GARY GURU: Just take it Miriam.

*(*MIRIAM *does.)*

GARY GURU: Good girl. Now, go on, stand still. If you really want to find him, you'll find the strength within you, to find him.

MIRIAM: But while I'm standing here, I'm wasting time.

GARY GURU: What is time? Does time really matter? Don't answer that, it won't be satisfying for either of us. *(He is gone.)*

———

(One hundred and thirty years have passed, GARY GURY, *eating a White Castle Slider, stands in front of* MIRIAM, *who is now crouched over like a very very old lady—perhaps now impossibly old, weak.)*

GARY GURU: These are better than Burger King but not as good as Wendy's. McDonalds is off the charts.

*(*MIRIAM *doesn't move.)*

GARY GURU: Oh, it's been a hundred and thirty years, you can move now.

(MIRIAM *does. We're back now in telepathy [voice overs].*)

GARY GURU: What have you learned?

MIRIAM: My body is a vessel for my soul.

GARY GURU: Yes.

MIRIAM: My soul is boundless.

GARY GURU: Yes.

MIRIAM: Fear is an illusion.

GARY GURU: Yes.

MIRIAM: There are no obstacles.

GARY GURU: Yes.

MIRIAM: I am power. I am strength. I am love. I am true.

GARY GURU: Yes.

MIRIAM: I want to drop my body.

GARY GURU: Drop it.

(MIRIAM *drops her body. This is a transformation. She is now somehow larger than life, her limbs extend, expand, she is more than human, she is boundless, epic, eternal.*)

(*We're no longer in telepathy.*)

GARY GURU: I love that color on you.

MIRIAM: Thanks. I think its inspired by something I once saw in an Yves Saint Laurent documentary.

GARY GURU: I've always been partial to Chloe, myself.

MIRIAM: To each their own. Speaking of which, in the late 80s Mcdonald's had this thing called a cheddar melt, which was their burger with melted cheese and grilled onions and I've never loved any burger more.

(*Beat*)

GARY GURU: You've learned well. You are ready. Now go.

(A great mountain appears.)

*(*MIRIAM *looks at the mountain and then spreads her arms and lifts elegantly off the ground.)*

*(*GARY GURY *watches as she disappears into the sky.)*

———

(Outside the SHE DOCTOR's *castle.)*

*(*MIRIAM *tastes the air.)*

MIRIAM: It does taste like Jolly Ranchers.

———

(Inside the SHE DOCTOR's *castle soon after.)*

*(*MIRIAM *faces the* SHE DOCTOR *who sits at her table spinning her spinning top. She doesn't look up, just plays with the top throughout.)*

SHE DOCTOR: So you're Miriam.

MIRIAM: Yes.

SHE DOCTOR: I didn't think you'd make it.

MIRIAM: You've been expecting me.

SHE DOCTOR: Of course I have.

MIRIAM: Where's David?

SHE DOCTOR: Sleeping.

MIRIAM: I want to see him.

SHE DOCTOR: You can't.

MIRIAM: I've come this far, I've traveled a great distance, persevered through time, faced obstacles, survived through self doubt, you can't stop me. I'm not afraid.

SHE DOCTOR: I didn't say you were.

MIRIAM: Why did you take him?

SHE DOCTOR: Because...

MIRIAM: Because why?

SHE DOCTOR: *(with a surprising and frightening strength)*

Because I could. And because you believed your love was true.

MIRIAM: It is true.

SHE DOCTOR: So you believe.

MIRIAM: I'm here aren't I?

SHE DOCTOR: Getting here is only half the battle. You still must get past me and then find David. And then still there's more after that. It never ends. There are just hills and valleys and mountains and oceans.

MIRIAM: I'll take it all as it comes. Will you stop playing with that fucking spinning top?

SHE DOCTOR: Make me.

MIRIAM: I will.

(The SHE DOCTOR stands up. The two look at each other.)

SHE DOCTOR: You're fun!

MIRIAM: Shut up.

(The MIRIAM and SHE DOCTOR.)

(It's a great battle.)

(A mixture of martial arts, hand to hand combat and futuristic Matrix type moves. There are no words, no soundtrack, just the sounds of two warriors battling.)

*(The battle is filled with ups and downs—*MIRIAM *looking just as much the winner as the loser. In the end* MIRIAM *through one quick, surprising move gets the upper hand and pins the* SHE DOCTOR *to the ground.)*

MIRIAM: Tell me where I can find David.

SHE DOCTOR: Find him yourself.

MIRIAM: I will…. I'm going to kill you now.

SHE DOCTOR: If you must.

MIRIAM: I must.

SHE DOCTOR: I should warn you—I'll be back. Sometime, somewhere, I'll gather enough strength and I'll return.

MIRIAM: I'll be waiting for you.

*(*MIRIAM *grabs the spinning top and shoves it into the* SHE DOCTOR*'s heart.)*

MIRIAM: Spin on this… Bitch.

SHE DOCTOR: *(With great joy as she dies)* You broke my heart.

(Afterwards)

MIRIAM: David?

———

(Lights up on a bedroom. DAVID *lying in the bed.* MIRIAM *rushes to him.)*

MIRIAM: David! I'm here.
I'm here now.
Wake up.
I'm here.
It's me, Miriam.
I'm here.

I've made it.
David. David. DAVID!

MIRIAM *shakes* DAVID. *He doesn't wake.*

———

(One hundred and three years later. We seem to be in a small apartment- DAVID *faces* MIRIAM.*)*

DAVID: You have to think outside the box!

MIRIAM: I'm not thinking inside the box but this apartment David *IS* a box! A tiny, suffocating box—just a kitchen! Nothing else. We can't live here. There's not even a bedroom! No living room! No place for either of us to get away from each other!

DAVID: Why would we ever want to get away from each other. We're in love! We're married! We're—

MIRIAM: Fuck off David.

DAVID: Miriam you don't have to be so—

MIRIAM: How can you even be trying to convince me of this! This is a stupid apartment! It's a stupid idiotic apartment! I hate this apartment. I HATE THIS APARTMENT!

DAVID: Miriam you're over-reacting.

MIRIAM: I am not!

DAVID: You are too. Look it's a really hot day and we've been looking at apartments for hours and—

MIRIAM: Don't try to calm me down.

DAVID: Come on, I'll buy you a cookie.

MIRIAM: Fuck off.

DAVID: Miriam.

MIRIAM: Fuck off! FUCK OFF!

(MIRIAM *runs out of the apartment and suddenly it turns into the desert.* DAVID *falls to the ground and* MIRIAM *rushes to him. Cradles his head in her lap*)

MIRIAM: That was the last time we spoke. That's so stupid. You know I didn't mean that. Well I did but I didn't really mean it. I should have at least said, I love you but fuck off. That would have been better. That would have been more what I meant. You know that. I know you do.
Remember that time we went up to the Cloisters for the day? We sat in that part of the park that over looked the Hudson…leaning against a tree, you were reading, I fell asleep listening to music. The day, time seemed endless, we were immortal, magical, you and me alone in the world, overlooking the trees, sheltered from the sun, the water glimmering, your eyes glimmering, my breath deep, my music melodic. Do you remember that David? Do you? If you don't, that's O K, when you wake up I'll tell you all of this again. I'll remind you of everything that we are and we'll move on. We'll continue, you and me.
Come on. Let's keep going.

(MIRIAM *picks* DAVID *up in her arms and starts to walk.*)

————

(*One hundred and eight years later. The two in what looks like a space ship both tied to their chairs.* HIRAM, *a carny, stands next to* MIRIAM's *chair.*)

HIRAM: You sure he's alright?

MIRIAM: He's fine. Rough night that's all.

HIRAM: Shoot, that's my middle name. Hiram "Rough Night" Hockney...

MIRIAM: Hiram?

HIRAM: Yeah, cool name right? Was named after some character in some book my mom read. I tried to read it but it was too long. So look it, you ever flown into space before?

MIRIAM: No.

HIRAM: You are in for something special I tell ya.

MIRIAM: I hope so. David loves space. The universe. We used to have a telescope. He'd spend hours looking at the stars, wondering about it all. He said it was his antidote.

HIRAM: Antidote? To what?

MIRIAM: I don't know really. Life, I guess...

HIRAM: Then he's gonna love this. Gets a little scary when you're breaking through the atmosphere but after that its pretty much smooth sailing.

MIRIAM: Alright.

HIRAM: Alright. Cool. So you both all tied in?

MIRIAM: Yes.

HIRAM: Safe travels.

(HIRAM *shuts the door. We hear the engine starting up.* MIRIAM *grabs* DAVID's *hand, squeezes tight.*)

———

(*Hours later.* MIRIAM *and* DAVID *in the space ship in deep space.* MIRIAM *kicks at the spaceship door trying to open it. She kicks and kicks, while she does—*)

MIRIAM: Open. OPEN. OPEN!!

(She kicks again, it gives.)

————

(18 years later. MIRIAM *and* DAVID *float through space,* DAVID *still unconscious,* MIRIAM *waiting. In the background we can see the solar system. Earth spinning on its axis.)*

*(*DAVID *opens his eyes, he sees* MIRIAM*. He smiles.)*

(Their eyes meet.)

DAVID: Hey.

MIRIAM: Hi.

DAVID: Are we in space?

MIRIAM: Yeah.

DAVID: Cool… Come here.

*(*MIRIAM *floats to* DAVID*.)*

DAVID: What happened?

MIRIAM: You were in an accident. You fell into a coma. *(She starts to cry.)*

DAVID: Hey, hey, its O K…

MIRIAM: Sometimes I wasn't sure if you were ever going to wake up.

DAVID: But I did. *(Beat. He touches her face, her hair.)*

MIRIAM: I'm sorry.

DAVID: For what?

MIRIAM: For telling you to fuck off.

DAVID: Oh. That. Yeah, you told me to fuck off, three times.

MIRIAM: Four. Four times.

DAVID: I knew you didn't mean it. Besides you were right.

MIRIAM: I know I was.

DAVID: Oh you do, do you?

(DAVID *smiles at* MIRIAM. *He knows her so well. She's overcome.*)

MIRIAM: Oh David, kiss me. Please. Hold me. Hold me as tight as you can. Hold me forever and don't ever let go. No matter what happens.
I'm just so glad you're awake.

(DAVID *and* MIRIAM *hug, tightly.*)

DAVID: Oh baby, I'm sorry it took me so long.

MIRIAM: I don't care. To speak to you again. To hold you again. I would have waited another thousand years if I had to.

(DAVID *and* MIRIAM *hold each other even tighter and then kiss as behind them thousands and thousands of couples are illuminated floating in space, holding each other tightly, kissing, becoming bright stars in space.*)

(*In the background, light illuminates the Earth and behind that, almost indiscernible, we see the* SHE DOCTOR. *She watches it all, content. She then takes the Earth in her hands like the spinning top toy she had at the beginning of the play and spins the Earth.*)

(*Light focuses on the Earth spinning, faster and faster and faster and faster as we—*)

(*Go to black*)

END OF PLAY

SECRET SONG from A Thousand Years

Grand Piano

Kenny Finkle

you wake up on the right side. You tell me to look

on the bright side. You hold me in your arms when I cry

you told me you'd be there when I die. You make me the most

delicious treats you always laugh when I complain about your feet

you think when I get angry its sweet. You told me you predicted

we'd meet. Where I leave off you pick up

when its empty you fill my cup why you do the things I'll

Never know That's just a secret that grows and grows

and grows and grows and grows.